MOTORCYCLES
A GUIDE TO THE WORLD'S BEST BIKES™

BMW
ULTIMATE RIDING EXPERIENCE

rosen publishing's
rosen central®

NEW YORK

RICHARD BARRINGTON

Published in 2014 by The Rosen Publishing Group, Inc.
29 East 21st Street, New York, NY 10010

Library of Congress Cataloging-in-Publication Data

Barrington, Richard, 1961–
BMW: ultimate riding experience/Richard Barrington.—First Edition.
    pages cm.—(Motorcycles: a guide to the world's best bikes)
Includes bibliographical references and index.
ISBN 978-1-4777-1857-5 (library binding)—ISBN 978-1-4777-1868-1 (pbk.)—
ISBN 978-1-4777-1869-8 (6-pack)
1. BMW motorcycle—Juvenile literature. I. Title.
TL448.B18B37 2014
629.227'5—dc23

2013013172

Manufactured in the United States of America

CPSIA Compliance Information: Batch #W14YA: For further information, contact Rosen Publishing, New York, New York, at 1-800-237-9932.

CONTENTS

INTRODUCTION

In the worlds of both automobiles and motorcycles, BMW is a name associated with excellence. The firm has pioneered new technologies while consistently producing machines that prove to be reliable over time. This pursuit of excellence is not engineering for its own sake; it is engineering geared to the purpose of enhancing the rider's experience.

In fact, BMW's slogan for its motorcycles is "the ultimate riding machine." Fans of other brands might argue in favor of their preferred bikes, but that's beside the point. Each manufacturer has its strengths and weaknesses, but BMW's slogan demonstrates the goal the company shoots for when it builds motorcycles. It aims high and has the rider in mind as much as the machine.

On the road, some other brands of motorcycles might be more immediately eye-catching, either because of their flashy sportiness or cool retro styling. BMWs, on the other hand, are not designed to fit in with anyone else's idea of what a motorcycle should look like. Across different categories of motorcycles, a consistent pattern is clear with BMWs. They tend to look solidly compact and often feature an eye-catching hump near the front formed by a large gas tank cover—a sign of the practical, utilitarian side of BMW's style.

The defining features of BMW bikes have been known for a great many years. Though certain features are updated periodically, the overall impression one gets is that the styling is somewhat timeless and uniquely BMW's.

This resource will give the reader a chance to see how BMW's engineering standards and design philosophy apply across several categories of motorcycles: sport, touring, roadster, enduro, and urban. By highlighting one BMW model from each of these categories, this resource will provide five examples of how the company strives to provide the ultimate riding experience to motorcycle enthusiasts of all types.

In 2013, BMW motorcycles celebrated its ninetieth anniversary. Ninety years is more than enough time to build a reputation, which BMW has certainly done. What's more important is that even with its proud history, BMW is not stuck in the past. It is forward-thinking and continues to innovate. This approach means riders will continue to prize BMW motorcycles for years to come.

BMW motorcycles have been combining distinctive styling with world-class engineering for over ninety years.

CHAPTER ONE

THE BMW S1000 RR: A RACER IN STREET CLOTHES

Superbikes are the athletes of the motorcycle world, built to combine power and agility. They are raced at a high level and attract an international following, with the Superbike World Championship featuring races in over a dozen countries spanning four different continents.

Besides having worldwide fan followings, superbikes are highly significant to manufacturers because the machines that race for the championship are based on production models that are available to the general public. Success on the racecourse can bring the kind of prestige that leads to higher sales. To put it more bluntly, winning in superbike racing gives a motorcycle company bragging rights.

Until recently, BMW had not been a major force in superbike racing, but that changed with the introduction of the BMW S1000 RR. This bike put BMW among the top competitors in superbike racing. Characteristically, BMW did it its own way.

Overall, the BMW S1000 RR has the pulse-quickening appearance people want from a sport bike, combined with some of the practical elements they expect from BMW. Even the color choices reflect this dual nature; owners can show their wild side with a bright red or blue color scheme or choose the more conservative grey or black options.

As is frequently the case with BMWs, the gasoline tank cover is one of the most prominent visible features of the BMW S1000 RR, rising from front to back before angling down again at a steeper angle in front of the seat, giving the rider a secure surface to lean against in the tilted-forward operating position characteristic of superbikes. Though the tail rises dramatically behind the rider, the rider's seat is neither as high nor as drastically forward-tilting as on some racing bikes, which is a note of moderation that conventional riders are likely to appreciate.

The S1000 RR has made BMW a force to be reckoned with in the Superbike World Championship, which is an elite international racing series.

BMW is a company known for technological leadership; superbike racing is a competition that calls for world-class levels of engineering refinement. Applying the high standards of BMW to the competitive world of superbike racing results in one of the most sophisticated high-performance motorcycles available on the market.

Reliable Power

The 999 cubic centimeter (61 cubic inch) engine of the BMW S1000 RR is at the smaller end of the range for superbikes. When it comes to sophisticated engineering though, size can be deceptive, and this power plant delivers an impressive 193 horsepower. A benefit of the modest engine size is that the bike has a dry weight of just 398 pounds (180 kilograms). The trade-off between power and weight is a key to both acceleration and top-end speed, and the BMW S1000 RR addresses this trade-off by packing a decent punch in a fairly lightweight machine.

The engine is liquid cooled and departs from many of its superbike peers by having four cylinders rather than the conventional two. The gearbox is six-speed, which has become something of a standard for conventional motorcycles these days. Fuel capacity is 4.6 gallons (17.4 liters), which would give the S1000 RR a cruising range of just under 190 miles (or just over 300 kilometers) at highway speeds.

The S1000 RR comes with an antilock braking system, which riders can fine-tune to their own preferences. It can

TRACK RECORD

The superbikes available to the general public are the basis for the machines raced in competition, most notably the Superbike World Championship. Because of this, performance in that championship can be a source of great pride to a model's manufacturers—and to the riders of that model.

On the racing front, BMW has proven that the S1000 RR can compete with the world's top motorcycles. BMW only officially entered the Superbike World Championship in 2009, and by 2012 finished second in the season-long manufacturers standings. This quick rise bodes well for BMW's future success in world-class superbike racing.

Another way to measure a bike against its peers is in reviewer ratings. Motorcycle.com runs an annual comprehensive comparison of superbikes called the Superbike Smackdown. This comparison involves having multiple reviewers ride several leading superbikes, which are then given scores based on a variety of criteria. These include ten subjective scoring categories, based on characteristics like handling and appearance, and ten measurable factors such as horsepower and price.

The BMW S1000 RR came out on top of Motorcycle.com's 2012 Superbike Smackdown, and the results weren't even close. BMW trounced the competition in the subjective categories and came in a close second based on measurable characteristics. The result was a clear win when the scores were combined.

Whether on the racetrack in the hands of world-class riders or on the test track in the hands of experienced reviewers, the BMW S1000 RR stacks up as one of the world's top superbikes. For riders who are up to the challenges of this category and are interested in buying the best, those successes make this bike well worth a test ride.

be operated in any one of four modes (rain, sport, race, and slick) or even disengaged for riders who like complete control over their braking.

Speed and Grace

Making a bike powerful is just part of the battle. Competition-level performance depends on the responsiveness of the bike in delivering that power, while everyday riding benefits from a smooth delivery of the bike's capabilities. The BMW S1000 RR is equipped to meet both these demands.

In addition to its high-performance credentials, the S1000 RR also has attention-getting styling.

A smooth gearbox and well-tuned power band are designed to make acceleration seem almost effortless through all six gears. In race or sport riding modes, throttle response is extremely sensitive—something high-level riders will appreciate, but it may come as a shock to those with a less competitive riding style. Fortunately, the rain or slick modes can be used to dampen down that sensitivity, making the ride feel more stable.

Braking is a strength of the S1000 RR, and in 2012 BMW sought to improve handling by shortening the wheelbase and adjusting the balance of the chassis. The latter refinement helps prevent the bike from leaning too heavily forward when braking hard or too heavily backward under heavy acceleration.

Besides being sensitive to a rider's needs in the physical aspects of its handling, the S1000 RR also delivers useful information. Racers will appreciate an indicator that tells the rider when lap speed is an improvement over prior laps. Street riders will appreciate a warning light that indicates when a desired preset speed is being exceeded. After all, a good superbike should provide speed, but it should also help its rider stay out of trouble.

Another example of how the S1000 RR is designed to keep the rider out of trouble is a wheelie detector that moderates acceleration when the front wheel is off the ground. Though wheelies are commonly thought of as stunts, they can be a source of handling problems in relatively

lightweight, high-torque bikes like the S1000 RR, so the electronic assistance of a wheelie detector may come in handy.

All in all, the S1000 RR stands up very well to the high standards of the superbike genre. Those standards are very demanding of both motorcycles and riders, so people buying this kind of bike need to understand the type of power and sensitivity they are taking on.

The raw power of the S1000 RR requires practiced and often subtle hands at the controls by even the most talented riders.

CHAPTER TWO

THE BMW K1600 GTL: SETTING A NEW STANDARD

motorcycle manufacturers produce different types of bikes to cater to different riding tastes, but also to fill a variety of roles in their marketing plans. Whereas superbikes are the flashy attention-getters that turn heads and pull customers into the showroom, a touring bike is the top-of-the-line model, a big-ticket item for consumers who want their bikes to come fully loaded.

From a rider's point of view, the purpose of a touring bike is to accommodate long trips. This means comfort for both rider and passenger, plenty of cargo space, and reliable power to haul a heavily laden machine. Agility is not a priority for these bikes; think of this as the heavyweight division of the motorcycle world. These machines are likely to weigh close to 1,000 pounds (453 kg) and pack engines ranging from 1,300 to 1,800 cubic centimeters (79.3 to 109.8 cu in). Smaller riders especially should take note—large touring bikes can be a handful for low-speed maneuvers, though they are smooth and luxurious when up to speed.

With the K1600 GTL, BMW has an extremely competitive entry into the large touring class of motorcycles. One look at it reveals some of the essential characteristics of a touring

RAISING THE BAR AT THE TOP OF THE LINE

Luxury touring bikes occupy a special place in a manufacturer's lineup. They are big, luxurious machines and have the price tags to match. Getting customers to fork over in excess of $20,000 for a motorcycle can be a nice boost to a manufacturer's revenues, and it takes a very special bike to do that.

Based on the reviews, the BMW K1600 GTL seems to be that type of special bike. It not only competes well in its category, but it may have set a new standard for high-end touring bikes. When discussing this category, credit should always be given to the Honda Gold Wing, which pretty much defined the genre. However, as the Gold Wing model has been getting on in years, perhaps it was time for somebody to redefine luxury touring. The BMW K1600 GTL seems to have done exactly that.

While superbikes get to compete on the racetrack, competition among touring bikes is largely left to the more subjective judgments of reviewers, and on that basis it is clear that BMW has a winner on its hands with the GTL. For riders, this bike is a best-of-both-worlds proposition: it provides all the benefits of size, with more power, comfort, amenities, and storage space than most bikes in the class, but at the same time it is relatively light and agile for the category, so the owner of a GTL does not have to completely abandon sport riding.

Typical of the high praise that this bike has earned was being named 2012 Motorcycle of the Year by *Rider* magazine. This means that the BMW K1600 GTL was not only tops in the luxury touring class, but it also beat out bikes from all manufacturers across all classes. That should be enough to put this model on the short list for anyone interested in a high-end touring bike.

bike: There is ample luggage space in side and center-back hard compartments, the rider's seat is wide and well-cushioned, and the passenger seat's wrap-around back makes it look almost like a small armchair.

Along with all these prerequisites of a big touring bike, the K1600 GTL also has distinctive BMW styling elements. Those visual touches are supported by the engineering and riding excellence that are even more essential to BMW's reputation.

Touring bikes like the K1600 GTL are built to make long trips more comfortable for the casual rider.

Built for the Long Haul

Touring bikes are intended to provide comfortable travel over long distances, and the BMW K1600 GTL is built to meet that goal in style. Naturally, this is a big bike: it weighs in at 708 pounds (321 kg) dry and can carry 467 pounds (212 kg) of load between rider, passenger, and luggage. Pulling such a load takes power, and the K1600 GTL supplies this with an in-line six-cylinder engine that actually measures 1,649 cubic centimeters (100.6 cubic inches). This engine is capable of delivering 160 horsepower via a six-speed gearbox and shaft drive.

Appropriately for a bike built for long cruises, the K1600 GTL features a sizable gas tank, with a capacity of 7 gallons (26.5 liters). Cruising at 55 miles per hour (88.5 km per hour), the K1600 GTL gets 51 miles to the gallon (21.7 km per liter). That combination of high fuel capacity with decent economy gives this bike an impressive highway cruising range of 357 miles (575 km).

Given the large engine, high fuel capacity, and substantial load tolerance, the K1600 certainly is not a small machine. With a total length of 98 inches (2,489 millimeters) and a width of 39.4 inches (1,000 mm), this is not a bike for squeezing in and out of tight spots. Still, even with all its size, the standard seat height is a reasonably accessible 29.5 inches (750 mm). For taller riders, a higher seat is available at no extra cost.

Anyone considering the K1600 GTL might also want to consider a closely related bike, the K1600 GT. The GTL is

BMW's legendary attention to detail can be seen in the styling elements of the K1600 GTL touring bike.

designed to be the ultimate in long-distance luxury cruising, while the GT moderates that opulence somewhat in favor of performance characteristics. For example, the GTL has a very laid-back seating position, while the GT leans the rider forward slightly into more of a sport-riding posture. Both share the same chassis and drive train, but the suspension on the GT is a little firmer. The GTL can carry a heavier load, but for stability reasons this requires that its speed be electronically limited. Still, at 136 miles per hour (219 km per hour), even that restricted speed is much more than most riders are likely to need.

Whether a rider chooses the GTL or the GT, what BMW has built for its top-of-the-line touring bikes are machines with the size to transport large loads over great distances in comfort and with the power to make doing so seem effortless.

Riding Experience

Because they are intended for extensive travel, touring bikes are judged on how they perform on the open road and how comfortable they are over long periods of time. The BMW K1600 GTL gets high grades from reviewers on those criteria, and the praise often centers on the engine. The in-line six-cylinder engine is so smooth, it behaves almost like a car engine. It idles gently but builds power responsively and gives this bike an impressive push when accelerating, plus the ability to maintain high speeds comfortably. A smoothly operating clutch and gearbox help this power to be applied evenly from low to high gears.

K1600 GTL owners can further smooth out the ride with optional dynamic traction control, which takes into account both wheel spin and lean angle in adjusting the application of power through the drive train. The ability to select three riding modes allows the rider to more specifically adjust the responsiveness of the bike to current road conditions.

BMW puts three brake discs, two up front and one on the rear wheel, at the rider's disposal to bring this large

The K1600 GTL's wide seats, ample luggage compartments, and protective fairing are all hallmarks of a bike built for long-range touring.

machine under control. These brakes give the K1600 GTL plenty of stopping power, while the antilock braking system allows that stopping power to be applied smoothly, without excessive front-end dive and without the bike being jarred off line.

While steering agility is an understandable sacrifice on a big bike, reviewers have found the K1600 GTL to be surprisingly nimble, with an intuitive lean into corners and a sharp return to the upright position when powering out of them. Riders who are looking for even sportier performance might want to consider the GT version, which has a tighter suspension and higher top speed.

Comfort is a consideration along with performance for touring bikes, and the K1600 GTL has amenities to make the ride feel pleasant and leisurely. These include heated grips and seat, cruise control, and an electronically adjustable windscreen.

All in all, the consensus on the K1600 GTL is that it hits all the right notes of comfort and smoothness for a luxury touring bike, but it throws in some surprisingly strong handling characteristics as well.

CHAPTER THREE

BMW R1200 R: A NEW BREED OF ROADSTER

Roadsters are one of the most venerable and versatile categories of motorcycle. They don't offer the performance extremes of superbikes or the luxury of touring bikes. Instead, they provide a little of everything, allowing them to function for everyday commuting, weekend cruising, and the occasional long trip.

BMW positions its R1200 R roadster as a "naked" bike, or something of a blank canvas that invites customization. Even in its basic form, the R1200 R is a roadster that incorporates some sport bike elements. The profile is dominated by a large gas tank that rises from back to front, one of the signature looks of BMWs. Up front, the conventional handlebars and round, single headlight fit the classic roadster mode, but elsewhere there are signs of a sportier personality. These include the black matte finish on the mirrors and other fixtures, and the tail of the bike, which is sharply tapered and sweeps upward dramatically.

For riders who want an especially striking look, BMW put out a special version to celebrate the company's ninetieth anniversary in 2013. This features a matte black finish throughout the bike, with special gold lettering and a gold-coated front fork. In a sense, this ninetieth-anniversary version sums

While it is essentially a roadster, the R1200 R also blends in some characteristics of a sport bike, such as the sleek design.

up what the R1200 R is all about: a bike that acknowledges the past, but that is engineered to be thoroughly modern.

Designed for Everyday Use

As befits a bike intended to be something of an all-around performer, the BMW R1200 R packs a decent amount of power into a modestly sized machine. The displacement of the four-cylinder, in-line engine measures 1,170 cubic centimeters (71.4 cu in), and this motor was upgraded in 2011

THE BEAUTY OF VERSATILITY

People are often attracted to roadsters for their looks. They represent a classic form of motorcycle styling, and stripped-down roadsters like the BMW R1200 R come across as elemental machines with a minimum of window dressing. However, beyond their classic beauty, there is a practical reason to love roadsters: versatility.

Many classes of motorcycles can be thought of as specialists: touring bikes for long journeys, superbikes for high performance, enduro bikes for off-road riding, etc. With these specialties, though, come limitations. Muscling a huge touring bike through stop-and-go traffic on short trips can quickly become tiresome. Superbikes are built for intensity rather than comfort, which can become wearing on longer rides. Enduro bikes can be ridden both on and off the road, but riders who spend their time exclusively on pavement will find their performance characteristics fairly limited.

Roadsters, on the other hand, are all-around machines, especially those that perform as well as the BMW R1200 R. Their moderate size makes them easy to handle in urban driving, while they also have enough punch and handling to be enjoyable on the open road. While not as luxurious as touring bikes, they are also comfortable enough for the occasional long trip.

All of this makes roadsters better suited for everyday riding than any of the specialist type of bikes. Their versatility also makes them a practical solution for riders who can afford to buy only one bike. On top of those practical benefits, there is also the issue of beauty. With their timeless looks, roadsters have an appeal that is not likely to fade as styling fashions come and go.

to expand maximum rpm to 8,500. This extra rev cushion comes in handy, as the engine's horsepower peaks at 7,500 rpm.

That peak performance produces 110 horsepower, which is more than adequate for the relatively light weight of the R1200 R: dry weight is just 448 pounds (203 kg). Notably, the permitted total weight of the R1200 R is more than twice that dry weight, which speaks well for the engine's muscle and gives the rider plenty of options for loading the bike up for long hauls or stripping it down for maximum performance.

Form meets function in BMW's motorcycles, such as in this 1200 R model, as meticulous engineering is packaged in timeless-looking bikes.

Another element of the R1200 R that is conducive to long trips is the cruising range. The 4.8-gallon (18-liter) gas tank is a healthy size for a roadster, and at a 55 miles-per-hour (88.5 km-per-hour) cruising speed, fuel economy is an impressive 57 miles per gallon (24.2 km per liter). Those figures combine to give this bike a cruising range of more than 273 miles (435 km) per tankful.

On the road, the R1200 R should handle most surfaces comfortably with an adjustable rear suspension and enough cushion in the front and back to handle the occasional bumps and potholes. Travel is 4.7 inches (120 mm) for the front wheel and 5.5 inches (140 mm) for the rear. Dual disc brakes in the front with a single disc brake in the rear help to keep everything under control.

In addition to standard equipment, BMW offers several accessories to help customize the R1200 R. These include both soft and hard-shell attachable luggage for those who want to take this roadster in a touring direction and styling highlights for those who want to emphasize its sportbike characteristics.

For the Love of the Open Road

One drawback to producing a solid, all-around machine is that it can be difficult to impress people in any one aspect of performance. However, critics have found plenty to love about the BMW R1200 R.

Part of the appeal of the R1200 R is that it packages modern engineering into a look that is classic, but not self-consciously retro. This allows the rider to enjoy the

Though it has been redesigned in recent years, the R1200 R already had built a track record as a reliable and responsive roadster.

aesthetics of a throwback roadster with the performance and reliability of a modern BMW. Just sitting on the bike provides hints at some of the modern touches. The instrument display combines traditional speed and tachometer dials with an LCD screen. The seat isn't flat as one might expect on an old-style roadster, but it is deeply scooped for comfort and lower-back support. Also, this is not a one-size-fits all bike; different seat heights are available to accommodate riders of different sizes and riding styles.

One cautionary note about the seating position: The engine of the R1200 R protrudes from either side of the bike to an unusual degree, and this can interfere with transferring legs from standing to riding position. However, this is the type of quirk riders generally get used to before long.

Getting up to speed, the R1200 R benefits from a firm front suspension and a low center of gravity that enhance stability at low speeds. That suspension also gives the R1200 R a sure-footed feel on rough road surfaces. The only drawback is that this firmness may give the rider's hands and seat an unwanted amount of jarring feedback from the road.

Once up to speed, the sportier characteristics of this roadster become clear. Cornering grip is excellent, and the responsive torque powers the bike confidently out of turns. That's not to say that the R1200 R has the straight-ahead speed of a sport bike, but its braking and handling do give it a high level of performance overall. In short, this is still very much a roadster, but one for people who ride as much for go as for show.

CHAPTER FOUR

BMW G650 GS: PAVEMENT OPTIONAL

Enduro bikes have some specific design necessities, but even those could not remove all the signature BMW elements from the appearance of the G650 GS. To some extent, it looks like a drastically thinned-down version of the R1200 R roadster, with the characteristic hump in front of the seat and bodywork that is both sleek and minimalist. However, the bright color schemes—the G650 GS is available in a sunny yellow and a crisp white—remind the onlooker that this bike is primarily built for fun.

For enduro bikes, fun means being ready for anything. Agility is the key to this category of motorcycle, as they are built to transition from highway to dirt to rock to mud and back again. With its slim build, tall carriage, and rugged components, the BMW G650 GS certainly fits the enduro bike profile, but it offers a little extra. The lines of the bike are sportier than one would expect from an enduro bike, and the saddle is less spartan. This is a bike that does not look out of place on paved roads, but at the same time shows enough agility to make pavement strictly optional.

BMW makes enduro bikes ranging in size from a 650 to a 1,200. Often with motorcycle fans, there is a "bigger is better" mentality, but when it comes to enduro bikes, "less is more" might be a better philosophy. After all, off-road riding can mean having to pick a bike back up somewhat regularly. That's why this section will focus on the smaller end of BMW's enduro line, on the G650 GS.

Ready for Anything

The agility necessary for an enduro bike can be seen in several aspects of the BMW G650 GS. With a dry weight of just 386 pounds (175 kg), the G650 GS can easily be

Enduro bikes are built with tall suspensions and heavy-duty shocks to help absorb the bumps of off-road riding.

handled through tight maneuvers and set back upright when necessary. Hand protectors and an aluminum engine guard are there to help rider and machine survive those occasional spills.

The bike's height, at 55 inches (1,390 mm) not counting the mirrors, allows it plenty of ground clearance. That height also allows the front and rear wheels a fair amount of travel; 6.7 inches (170 mm) of give in the front and 5.5 inches (140 mm) in the rear will help the bike negotiate the deep ruts and jutting rocks of dirt roads and trails.

The versatility of enduro bikes allows riders to tackle a wide variety of often extreme conditions for the more adventurous rider.

Still, not all the design of the G650 GS is devoted to off-road riding. Though the single-cylinder, 652 cubic centimeter (39.8 cubic inch) engine generates only a modest 50 horsepower, the bike's light frame makes that enough to push top speed above 100 miles per hour (160 km per hour). One compensation of that smaller engine is the impressive 74 miles-per-gallon (31.5 km-per-liter) fuel economy at cruising speed. Even with a smallish 3.7-gallon (14-liter) tank, that's enough to give the G650 GS a respectable amount of range.

Other elements that show the G650 GS respects the pavement as well as the dirt road include an adjustable suspension that can lower the bike's height. Also, the seat height is not too extreme to begin with, at 31.5 inches (800 mm), though a higher seat is available to accommodate taller riders.

The design of the G650 GS makes it rugged and agile enough to ride off-road but practical enough to ride on pavement. Overall, this bike is designed to be ready for anything.

A Sure-Footed Ride

The G650 GS won't wow you with its acceleration, but balance is more the goal of an enduro bike than speed. While there are no thrilling peaks to the power curve, a responsive clutch makes getting underway seem effortless, and the bike accelerates smoothly through all five gears. However, being a single-cylinder engine with a five-speed gearbox, riders should expect that it will labor a little at higher speeds.

ON OR OFF THE ROAD

Anyone who plans to spend a substantial amount of time riding off the pavement has a fundamental choice to make: motocross or enduro bike?

The hybrid nature of the G650 GS is typical of enduro bikes. They are designed to perform competently on both dirt and pavement, and unlike motocross bikes, they are street legal. Motocross bikes perform better on loose surfaces, providing better grip, lighter frames for maneuverability, and stiff suspensions built for maximum shock absorption. However, owning a bike that can handle a little of the rough stuff but still feel comfortable on the road has its advantages as well.

Except for people who have a great deal of property or happen to live right by a dirt bike trail, owning a motocross bike means needing a car and a trailer to get the bike where it can be ridden. It also means owning a second bike if the rider wants to do any cruising or simply use a motorcycle for transportation.

In contrast, the all-around abilities of enduro bikes mean they can be ridden to the trail and back again. Their easy maneuverability also makes them a useful commuter vehicle during the workweek. In addition, a bike like the G650 GS has characteristics that can accommodate some longer trips as well, such as excellent gas mileage, decent top speed, and even a luggage rack with attachable hard side cases available as accessories.

So, motocross or enduro bike? In choosing, riders would do well to consider all their needs, and not just their off-road plans.

The upright seating and wide handlebars position the rider to feel very much in control for tight maneuvers. The feeling of balance is enhanced by the bike's low center of gravity, due in part to an under-seat gas tank.

Overall, the G650 GS is a hybrid by nature. One example is the brakes, which come standard with an antilock system that can be turned off when riding on dirt, since riders often want a more in-touch feel under those circumstances. As a hybrid, the G650 GS is not a standout on the highway nor could it be described as a hard-core dirt bike. However, for riders who plan to incorporate a bit of both conditions into their travels, this is a bike that will take the changes in stride.

CHAPTER FIVE

THE BMW C650 GT: LIFE IN THE BIG CITY

In reviewing different styles of motorcycles, it is helpful to think of them as different kinds of tools, each designed to do a specific job. In the case of the BMW C650 GT, that job is primarily urban transportation, but with some extras thrown in as well.

BMW describes the C650 GT as a "maxi-scooter," and it is clear why it makes the "maxi" distinction. The C650 GT looks a bit like a hybrid between a scooter and a touring bike. The scooter elements are clearest in the low height, small wheels, and upright seating position. On the other hand, with its wide faring and adjustable windscreen, this bike has elements that were designed with the open road in mind. The engine is about two or three times the size one would need for simply putting around town, and the seat is built to be comfortable for more than just short commutes and errands.

The BMW C650 GT has the stylishly urban appearance of a scooter, though with more of a nod to aerodynamic elements than on slower-paced machines. It has the compact size to deal with the tight traffic and limited parking typical of a big city, but it has an engine and suspension that can keep up on the highway as well. What all this adds up to is a machine that is suited for the demands of urban riding, but not limited to those conditions.

IS A SCOOTER REALLY A MOTORCYCLE?

Scooters have been an established form of urban transportation for decades, especially in Europe. Whether or not scooters should be classified as true motorcycles depends on one's perspective—and on the scooter in question.

Similar to how living things evolve, machines have a tendency to adapt to their surroundings. In the case of scooters, the urban environment has caused them to evolve as simpler, lighter, and lower-to-the ground machines than the motorcycles typically seen cruising the highways.

As to whether this change has specialized scooters too much to be called motorcycles, the question should not be asked based on appearances alone. After all, comparing touring bikes with enduro bikes, or superbikes with roadsters makes it clear that motorcycles come in all kinds of shapes and sizes. Looks may be one factor, but how well a machine holds up to the title of motorcycle depends on performance.

In the case of the BMW C650 GT, the engine size, responsiveness, and handling all help this bike make a claim to be a true motorcycle. On the other hand, riders looking for a full motorcycling experience will miss the clutch and gearshifts. Still, for a rider who wants a bike that can be useful as urban transportation during the workweek, and then stretched out a bit on the open road over the weekend, the C650 GT is enough like both a scooter and a motorcycle to successfully bridge those two worlds.

Low-Key Power

Although the BMW C650 GT has the basic shape of a scooter, the technical specifications underscore some important differences. While the 15-inch (381-mm) wheels are on the small side, the suspension allows for a surprisingly generous 4.5 inches (114 mm) of travel in both front and back. This suspension contributes to an overall height of 55.6 inches (1,411 mm); perhaps surprisingly, this would put the C650

The BMW C650 GT has the compact size of a scooter, but it also has an aerodynamic design geared toward the open road.

GT somewhere between BMW's roadster and touring bikes in total height.

The C650 GT not only stands tall, but it has some heft to it. Its dry weight is 549 pounds (249 kg), which is a far cry from the lightweight image of the typical scooter. In part, that weight can be attributed to the size of the engine. Scooters sometimes come with engines smaller than 100 cubic centimeters (6.1 cu in). In that world, a 200 cubic centimeter (12.2 cu in) engine is considered large, so the C650 GT's 647 cubic centimeter (39.5 cu in) displacement would be practically off the charts.

The payoff for this extra engine size is a top speed in excess of 100 miles per hour (161 km per hour). Clearly, the C650 GT was designed to do more than simply go from stoplight to stoplight, but because it still retains the outward characteristics of an urban scooter, this bike is a good example of low-key power.

A Scooter with a Motorcycle's Heart

Anyone used to the simplicity of a scooter will not feel out of place on the BMW C650 GT. Despite having a full motorcycle-sized engine, the BMW operates like a scooter in fundamental respects. The brake controls are both on the handlebars, rather than the usual motorcycle arrangement of front brake on the handlebars and rear brake by the right footpeg. The handlebars can accommodate both brakes because there is

Motorcycle or scooter? The BMW C650 GT combines the power of a motorcycle with the simplicity and smaller size of a scooter.

no clutch or gears to shift, another characteristic more typical of scooters than motorcycles.

These ease-of-use features are not just useful to less experienced riders. In tight urban traffic, the constant series of shifts necessary on a traditional motorcycle can quickly become tiresome, so a simpler approach allows the rider to concentrate just on throttle and brakes.

Upon twisting the throttle, riders will get a feel for the motorcycle's heart that powers this scooter. Compared to the typical scooter, the response is more immediate, acceleration

The compact size of the C650 GT makes it well suited for the limited parking options of urban areas.

sharper, and top speed higher. The C650 GT also allows riders to handle curves with a high degree of confidence.

Fuel economy is respectable, at 53 miles-per-gallon (22.5 km-per-liter) when the bike is up to highway speeds, though it is likely to be considerably less in stop-and-go city traffic. With a 4.2-gallon (16-liter) gas tank, the C650 GT's fuel economy gives it a range of over 200 miles (322 km). Along with the bike's performance characteristics, this cruising range allows the C650 GT to be enjoyed both inside and outside city limits.

SPECIFICATION CHART

S1000 RR

Displacement	999 cc / 61 cin
Wheelbase	1,422 mm / 56.0 in
Horsepower	193 hp @ 13,000 rpm
Torque	83 lb-ft @ 9,750 rpm
Transmission	6-speed
Fuel Capacity	4.6 gallons / 17.4 liters

K1600 GTL

Displacement	1649 cc / 100.6 cin
Wheelbase	1,680 mm / 66.1 in
Horsepower	160 hp @ 7,750 rpm
Torque	129 lb-ft @ 5,250 rpm
Transmission	6-speed
Fuel Capacity	7 gallons / 26.5 liters

R1200 R

Displacement	1,170 cc / 71.4 cin
Wheelbase	1,495 mm / 58.9 in
Horsepower	110 hp @ 7,500 rpm
Torque	88 lb-ft @ 6,000 rpm
Transmission	6-speed
Fuel Capacity	4.8 gallons / 18 liters

G650 GS

Displacement	652 cc / 39.8 cin
Wheelbase	1,477 mm / 58.2 in
Horsepower	50 hp @ 6,500 rpm
Torque	44 lb-ft @ 5,000 rpm
Transmission	5-speed
Fuel Capacity	3.7 gallons / 14 liters

C650 GT

Displacement	647 cc / 39.5 cin
Wheelbase	1,591 mm / 62.6 in
Horsepower	60 hp @ 7,500 rpm
Torque	49 lb-ft @ 6,000 rpm
Transmission	Continuously Variable Transmission
Fuel Capacity	4.2 gallons / 16 liters

GLOSSARY

AERODYNAMIC Consisting of a design that allows air to efficiently flow past the body of a motorcycle.

ANTILOCK BRAKING A system that automatically eases back on brake pressure when it senses a wheel is locking up and then reapplies it once the wheel is rotating again. A locked wheel can increase stopping distances and cause a bike to lose stability.

CLUTCH A mechanism generally operated by a lever on a motorcycle's handlebars, the clutch is used to disengage and re-engage the engine from the drive train, for the purpose of changing gears.

CRUISING RANGE The total distance a bike can travel on one tank of gas. This is a function of each bike's fuel economy and gas tank capacity.

DISPLACEMENT The combined interior volume of a bike's engine cylinders, a standard measurement of an engine's effective size.

ENDURO BIKE A motorcycle designed to be agile and durable enough to be operated on dirt roads and yet having characteristics that make it appropriate (and legal) for operation on paved surfaces as well.

LIQUID COOLED A system that uses oil, coolant, or other fluids to flow around an engine to keep it from overheating.

MOTOCROSS BIKE A motorcycle designed to be ridden exclusively on unpaved surfaces, that generally lack lights and other equipment that would make it street legal.

NAKED BIKE A motorcycle with very little in the way of bodywork, allowing a clear view of the frame and engine.

ROADSTER A motorcycle with classic looks and minimal bodywork and accessories designed for all-around street operation.

SCOOTER A compact motorized two-wheeler with a small engine and simplified controls, designed for short-distance transportation, especially in urban areas.

SHAFT DRIVE A method of transferring engine power to the rear wheel by means of a rotating shaft, rather than via a chain or belt.

SUPERBIKE A high-performance racing motorcycle that is also commercially available for street use.

SUSPENSION TRAVEL The amount of compression allowed in a motorcycle's front- or rear-wheel suspension for the purpose of absorbing shocks from uneven road surfaces.

TACHOMETER A gauge on a motorcycle that measures the engine speed, usually represented as RPM (revolutions per minute).

THROTTLE A mechanism for regulating the flow of fuel to an engine, and thus controlling the amount of power being applied. On a motorcycle, this is generally operated by twisting the right handgrip.

TORQUE A measure of applied force, which helps indicate a motorcycle's power of acceleration.

TOURING BIKE A large bike built for long-range travel and therefore designed with an emphasis on comfort, carrying capacity, and smooth operation at highway speeds.

WHEELBASE A measure of a motorcycle's length, which can impact maneuverability. It is the distance from the center of the front wheel to the center of the back wheel.

FOR MORE INFORMATION

American Motorcyclist Association
13515 Yarmouth Drive
Pickerington, OH 43147
(800) 262-5646
Web site: http://www.americanmotorcyclist.com
This association organizes motorcycle events and promotes
   the interests of motorcycle owners.

BMW Motorcycle Owners of America
P.O. Box 3982
Ballwin, MO 63022
(636) 394-7277
Web site: http://www.bmwmoa.org
This volunteer organization fosters friendship and a sense
   of community among BMW motorcycle owners and clubs
   throughout the United States.

BMW Riders Association
P.O. Box 599
Troy, OH 45373
(866) 924-7102
Web site: http://www.bmwra.org
This is a community that allows BMW riders from around the
   world to exchange ideas and experiences.

Canadian Motorcycle Association
605 James Street North, 4th Floor
Hamilton, ON L8L1J9
Canada
(905) 522-5705

Web site: http://www.canmocycle.ca
This association is dedicated to promoting the interests of
motorcycle riders in Canada.

Canadian Motosport Racing Corporation
P.O. Box 1466
Stouffville, ON L4A 8A3
Canada
(905) 642-5607
Web site: http://www.cmracing.com
This organization oversees off-road motorcycle racing in
Canada.

Motorcycle Safety Foundation
2 Jenner Street, Suite 150
Irvine, CA 92618
(949) 727-3227
Web site: http://www.msf-usa.org
This not-for-profit organization is geared toward advancing
rider education and training.

WEB SITES

Due to the changing nature of Internet links, Rosen Publishing has developed an online list of Web sites related to the
subject of this book. This site is updated regularly. Please use
this link to access the list:

http://www.rosenlinks.com/MOTO/BMW

FOR FURTHER READING

Allen, Laurel C., and Mark Gardiner. *BMW Racing Motorcycles: The Mastery of Speed*. Center Conway, NH: Whitehorse Press, 2008.

Cloesen, Uli. *BMW Custom Motorcycles: Choppers, Cruisers, Bobbers, Trikes & Quads*. Poundbury, Dorchester, UK: Veloce, 2011.

DK Publishing. *Motorcycle: The Definitive Visual History*. New York, NY: DK Publishing, 2012.

Gantriis, Peter. *The Art of BMW: 90 Years of Motorcycle Excellence*. Minneapolis, MN: Motorbooks, 2013.

Holmstrom, Darwin. *BMW Motorcycles*. Minneapolis, MN: Motorbooks, 2009.

Hough, David L. *Proficient Motorcycling: The Ultimate Guide to Riding Well*. Irvine, CA: BowTie Press, 2008.

Klancher, Lee. *Motorcycle Dream Garages*. Minneapolis, MN: Motorbooks, 2009.

Lewis, Jack. *Coming and Going on Bikes: Essaying the Motorcycle*. Seattle, WA: Litsam, Inc., 2010.

Masi, C. G. *How to Set Up Your Motorcycle Workshop: Tips and Tricks for Building and Equipping Your Dream Workshop*. Center Conway, NY: Whitehorse Press, 2010.

McKechnie, Gary. *Great American Motorcycle Tours*. Berkeley, CA: Avalon Travel Publishing, 2006.

Riding America's Back Roads: 20 Top Motorcycle Tours, Roadrunner Motorcycle Touring & Travel. East Petersburg, PA: Chapel Publishing, 2010.

Walker, Mick. *Motorcycle: Evolution, Design, Passion*. Baltimore, MD: The Johns Hopkins University Press, 2006.

BIBLIOGRAPHY

Adams, Bradley. "2012 BMW S 1000 RR Reworked Royalty/ First Ride." Sport Rider. Retrieved March 2012 (http://www.sportrider.com).

Ash, Kevin. "BMW R1200R Classic Review." Ash on Bikes. Retrieved January 4, 2013 (http://www.ashonbikes.com).

BMW Motorrad USA. "G 650 GS, Technical data." Retrieved January 7, 2013 (http://www.bmwmotorcycles.com/us/en).

Dawes, Justin. "2012 Superbike Smackdown IX Street Conclusion." Motorcycle USA. Retrieved June 11, 2012 (http://www.motorcycle-usa.com).

Duke, Kevin. "2011 BMW G650GS Review." Motorcycle. Retrieved November 18, 2011 (http://www.motorcycle.com).

FIM Superbike. "Supersport World Championships & FIM Superstock 1000cc Cup." WorldSBK.com. Retrieved January 15, 2013 (http://www.worldsbk.com).

MotorcycleNews.com. "BMW G650GS." Retrieved January 7, 2013 (http://www.motorcyclenews.com).

Rider magazine staff. "*Rider* Magazine's 2012 Motorcycle of the Year." *Rider*. Retrieved July 3, 2012 (http://www.ridermagazine.com).

Simona. "2011 BMW R 1200 R and R 1200 R Classic." Top Speed. Retrieved November 1, 2010 (http://www.topspeed.com).

WorldSBK.com. "2012 Standings Manufacturers–FIM Superbike World Championship." Retrieved December 28, 2012 (http://www.worldsbk.com).

WorldWideMotorcycles.com. "Buying a Motorcycle Guide Part 3—Enduro Motorcycles and Motocross Bikes." Retrieved January 7, 2013 (http://worldwidemotorcycles.com).

INDEX

About the Author

Richard Barrington is an avid motorcyclist with nearly two decades of riding experience. His favorite rides are in the Finger Lakes region of New York State. When not riding motorcycles he is a senior financial analyst for MoneyRates.com. His articles have been syndicated on MSN.com, the *Huffington Post*, and Forbes.com. He has appeared on National Public Radio's *Talk of the Nation* and American Public Media's *Marketplace*. He graduated from St. John Fisher College with a B.A. in communications and earned his Chartered Financial Analyst designation from the CFA Institute.

Photo Credits

Cover, p. 1 Racefotos2008/Shutterstock.com; pp. 5, 12 Fast Bikes Magazine/Future/Getty Images; p. 7 Maxim Shipenkov/EPA/Landov; pp. 10, 38 © AP Images; p. 15 © Jan Woitas/DPA/ZUMA Press; pp. 17, 19 Charles Chen Art/Shutterstock.com; p. 22 miker/Shutterstock.com; p. 24 Mario Vedder/dapd/AP Images; p. 26 © Oleksiy Maksymenko/Alamy; pp. 29, 30 Kevin Wing Photography; p. 36 Raymond Boyd/Michael Ochs Archives/Getty Images; p. 39 BSA/ZOJ WENN Photos/Newscom; interior pages background elements Dudarev Mikhail/Shutterstock.com, Yuriy_fx/Shutterstock.com; back cover © iStockphoto.com/JordiDelgado.

Designer: Brian Garvey; Editor: Nicholas Croce;
Photo Researcher: Amy Feinberg